DEMIAN

NOTES

including
- *Life and Background*
- *Introduction to* Demian
- *List of Characters*
- *Critical Commentaries*
- *Character Analyses*
- *Review Questions*
- *Selected Bibliography*

D1826655

by
Bruce L. Marcoon, M.Ed.
English Department
Upper Darby Senior High School

Cliffs® Notes
INCORPORATED
LINCOLN, NEBRASKA 68501

Editor	Consulting Editor
Gary Carey, M.A.	*James L. Roberts, Ph.D.*
University of Colorado	*Department of English*
	University of Nebraska

ISBN 0-8220-0385-6
© Copyright 1974
by
C. K. Hillegass
All Rights Reserved
Printed in U.S.A.

1988 Printing

Cliffs Notes, Inc.   Lincoln, Nebraska

CONTENTS

Life and Background

Hermann Hesse was born in the little south German village of Calw on July 2, 1877. Situated on the edge of the Black Forest, Calw was to become the colorful setting of much of Hesse's writing. Hesse was the son of Johannes Hesse, who had been a missionary for the Lutheran Pietists to India. Forced to return to Europe after a short stay in India, Johannes worked in, and helped establish, a religious publishing house in Calw. Hermann's maternal grandfather, Hermann Gundert, also spent a major portion of his life as a missionary in India, acquiring a huge library of books about Eastern thought and becoming a master of Indic languages.

As a child, Hesse was greatly subjected to religious influences, both to the narrower views of Protestantism as well as to the wider scope of the Eastern religions and philosophies. Both views never left him; they became an integral part of his thought. His house in Calw was frequently the scene of visitations from foreigners, ranging from Buddhists to Americans. At his disposal was his grandfather's rich library. Hesse himself much later stated that all of his writing was religious in nature, not in the orthodox sense, but in a larger, universal way.

It was established early that Hesse would become a theological student. While showing intellectual promise as a student, young Hesse disliked school, especially the rigidity and the stifling of creativity of the German educational system of his time. His grades were never outstanding, and he disliked his teachers. He once stated that he had had only one teacher whom he liked. His reaction to this oppressive atmosphere is also reflected in his writings, especially in the bitter attack in *Unterm Rad (Beneath the Wheel)*. By the age of thirteen, Hesse had decided that he was going to be a poet. Great stress caused him to flee the Maulbronn Seminary, the setting of Mariabronn in *Narcissus and Goldmund.* He became so despondent that he considered suicide and a pistol for that end was purchased.

Causing great concern to his parents, Hesse was subjected to a variety of remedies for his rebelliousness. These ranged from a school for the disturbed to an attempt at exorcism. In 1894, Hesse became an apprentice in Perrot's tower clock factory in Calw. Needless to say, this was not satisfactory to him. Some progress was made in 1895 when he became an apprentice in the book trade in Heckenhauer's bookstore in Tubingen, although Hesse was still a rebel. A few years later he served in a similar capacity in Basel, from where he traveled through Switzerland and to Italy.

After writing a few minor works, Hesse achieved recognized literary success in 1904 with the publication of *Peter Camenzind,* a very popular book written in the tradition of the German Romanticists. In the same year he married Maria Bernoulli, and the couple took up a secluded residence at Gaienhofen, where Hesse became a free lance writer and a contributor to a number of journals.

Hesse's second successful novel, *Unterm Rad (Beneath the Wheel)* was published in 1906, followed by *Gertrud* in 1910 and *Rosshalde* in 1914. The latter work strongly depicts the plight of the temperamental artist and his wife. Meanwhile, Hesse had become associated with the pacifist Romain Rolland and had been writing numerous essays against the growing nationalism of the German people. Many of these writings have been translated into English and are available in a volume entitled *If the War Goes On....* The publication of *Knulp* in 1915 includes three stories about the life of a colorful vagabond.

A turning point in Hesse's life occurred in 1916 when his father's death, coupled with the illnesses of his son Martin and his wife, forced Hermann to seek refuge in a Lucerne sanatorium. His condemnation by his native Germany for his pacifistic views probably compounded his already serious problems. In 1916-17 Hesse had more than seventy sessions with a psychologist, J. B. Lang, who was a disciple of the famous Carl Gustav Jung. Supposedly these were more friendly conversations than attempts at serious psychoanalysis. The result was favorable for Hesse and of great importance to his future writings. The works following this period, beginning with *Demian*, cannot be fully understood without a recognition of the Jungian influence. Following *Demian* were *Marchen* (reprinted in English as *Strange News from Another Star*) and *Klingsor's Last Summer*, a collection of three excellent novellas, originally containing *Siddhartha*. At the same time, Hesse became co-editor of the newspaper *Vivos Voco* and decided to move, alone, to Montagnola. In 1920, he produced *Blick ins Chaos* which was referred to by T. S. Eliot in *The Wasteland*.

Hesse divorced his wife and adopted Swiss citizenship in 1923. He then married Ruth Wegner the following year. The years 1924-27 saw the publication of some of Hesse's best autobiographical pieces, namely *Kurgast* (1924), and *Die Nurnberger Reise* (1927), as well as his second divorce, which is reflected upon in *Der Steppenwolf* (1927). *Narcissus and Goldmund* was published in 1930, and shortly thereafter Hesse married Ninon Dolbin, who was to remain his companion until his death. In 1932, Hesse published *Die Morgenlandfahrt (The Journey to the East)*. The only other major novel to be produced was *The Glass Bead Game (Magister Ludi)*, which was published in 1943. Hesse was awarded the Nobel Prize in 1946.

During the course of World War II, Hesse was to relive the nightmare of World War I. Once again he became the subject of German ostracism because of his anti-nationalistic views. Following the war, however, his writings again became popular in Germany and have remained so until relatively recent times. After receiving many literary honors, Hermann Hesse died in seclusion of a cerebral hemorrhage in Montagnola on August 9, 1962.

Of immediate concern is the Hesse phenomenon now existent in the United States. Hesse's works have long enjoyed popularity outside of Germany, especially in southern Europe and Latin America. Indeed, of twentieth-century German writers, only Thomas Mann and Franz Kafka have been written about more than Hesse. However, Hesse has remained almost virtually unknown in the United States until the last decade. Only a handful of his works had been translated into English, and some of those had been very poor translations. Very few critical articles or references appeared in literary publications prior to the Nobel Prize of 1946. For a short time afterwards, his name was mentioned more frequently and some worthwhile critical material appeared. Largely though, Hesse was known only to a handful of individuals on college campuses. Hesse himself doubted greatly that he would ever receive popular recognition in the English-speaking world, particularly the United States.

Within the last ten years, Hesse has been worshiped by many college students who have made him a cult hero. *Siddhartha* and *Demian,* particularly, are now found in the curricula of some of the more progressive high schools. Ironically, *Siddhartha* is, among other things, one of the greatest criticisms of formal education that one could read, which is one aspect which makes it so appealing to today's alienated students. The novel has recently been adapted into a motion picture.

The reasons for Hesse's current popularity stem from several factors. Initially, his wide-spread acceptance in the United States was due to the youth culture which identified with his alienated protagonists. Both a rock group and a California discotheque owe their names to *Steppenwolf,* which has become a virtual Bible for the counter-culture. Also, a record album has been entitled "Abraxas," after the Gnostic deity who is an integral part of *Demian.* Youths frequently hear themselves echoed when Harry Haller condemns pre-World War II German society for building a dehumanizing military industrial complex and for destroying nature. When Haller uses drugs to achieve a state of intense awareness, they identify again, not realizing how little this aspect has to do with the essence of the novel. This generation, a great many of whom were witnesses to their country's involvement in what they considered to be an unjustifiable, immoral war (Viet Nam), found a spokesman against chauvinistic nationalism in Hesse. Today, when they see "progress" as a threat to the individual values and soul, they question the process deeply, as did Hesse. These individuals identify with the author in his own plight and have "turned within" to find their way. Hesse himself said that each of his writings was, in a sense, a spiritual autobiography. From the Nietzschean view of *Demian*, which questions the "herd instinct" and the "mass morality," to the concept of individual sacrifice for the sake of helping another person achieve a higher level of existence as depicted in the futuristic *Glass Bead Game (Magister Ludi)*, inspiration has been given and guidelines established.

Hesse, now the subject of much discussion, has been both highly praised and severely condemned. Whether he is a saint or whether his writings are just another fad certain to be forgotten remains to be seen. Because he deals with very real issues which are sensitive in our society today, he is rarely spoken of objectively. Because of conflicts in personal viewpoints, much of the intrinsic merit of his works has been neglected and not examined closely enough by both those of the "establishment" and those who seek to identify with Charles Reich's concept of "Consciousness III."

Introduction to "Demian"

Published in 1919, *Demian* is a crucial novel to an understanding of Hermann Hesse and his current popularity in the United States. *Demian*, whose title came to Hesse in a dream, is the direct outgrowth of his psychoanalysis of 1916-17. It marks a new direction in both the tone and message of his works. Dr. Timothy Leary has referred to Hermann Hesse as "the poet of the interior journey." *Demian* is the beginning of Hesse's introspection and his turning to the "inward way," as well as his discovery of "magical thinking" as answers to the dilemmas presented to us by modern life.

In its format, *Demian* could be classified as a *Bildungsroman,* a novel of education, popular in Germany's era of Romanticism. But, by combining with this traditional approach the surrealistic quality of "magical thinking," Hesse has far transcended the typical novel of this type. "Magical thinking" is a term difficult to define and would possibly be best handled by an example.

In a short, autobiographical essay, Hesse looked to the future and pictured himself in a jail cell for some act of immorality. In order to pass the time, he began painting a picture on the wall of the cell. (Painting was Hesse's life-long love.) In the picture there is a train travelling into a dark tunnel. Hesse imagines himself jumping onboard the train, going through the tunnel, thus escaping his captors. Somehow, this is the essence of his "magical thinking."

The combination of traumas of 1916-18 caused Hesse great mental anguish. His rejection by Germany, his father's death, and the illnesses of his wife and his son Martin caused Hesse to seek the aid of J. B. Lang, an associate of the famous psychologist Carl Gustav Jung. More than seventy sessions took place between Lang and Hesse from 1916 to 1917. One result was that Hesse began to reexamine his whole system of values and to formulate a new one. All of his novels subsequent to *Demian* reflect his new thinking and his increased awareness of the workings of the human mind. The latter aspect becomes more obvious after 1919, although it seems that even in his earlier works Hesse was intuitively aware, though not formally schooled, in such matters. After 1919, one cannot fully understand or appreciate Hesse without a knowledge of such terms as "unconscious," *anima,* and "archetype."

Demian was produced within two months' time in what one biographer and personal acquaintance of Hesse refers to as a "white heat." It was published under the pseudonym Emil Sinclair. One reason for the use of the pen name was the disfavor toward Hesse in Germany at the time. Had the novel been published under his real name, it would have been ignored. Under this guise, however, it was not only a success, but Sinclair was also awarded the Fontane Prize for new authors. Soon the truth became known through a careful style analysis. Hesse could not accept the prize, the monetary value of which he could have used, because he was already an established author. Even his friend, the renown Thomas Mann, could not believe that this was the work of Hermann Hesse, so radical was his departure from his earlier work.

Structurally, *Demian* is the beginning of a pattern followed in all of Hesse's novels after 1919. The book falls loosely into three sections. The first of these deals with the protagonist's awareness of an inharmonious world and some action which causes the loss of his innocence and can be paralleled with the biblical fall from grace. The second section, which is the longest, concerns itself with the period of anguish and despair which follows the fall. The third portion contains some degree of enlightenment for the protagonist. In one manner or other, he learns to come to terms with his life and with himself. However, this is not a permanent state and it can be assumed that the protagonist is able to achieve the heights of intense awareness and harmony only periodically, but, nevertheless, he is able to continue his existence in an easier manner than most people because he has occasionally tasted complete harmony. The only novel of Hesse's in which the protagonist both attains and maintains this concept of Nirvana is, appropriately enough, *Siddhartha.*

List of Characters

Emil Sinclair

The youthful protagonist of the novel who, in course of ten years, falls from childhood innocence, suffers great anguish in his search for self understanding, and finally achieves the awareness for which he has been striving.

Max Demian

A youth several years older than Sinclair who acts as Emil's guide in his search for fulfillment. Demian's name parallels his function; he is Sinclair's *daemon* or inner spirit. His function and human superiority is further related to his first name, as it is possibly a shortened form of "maximus." Demian and his actions frequently cannot be rationally explained as he is the product of "magical thinking."

Frau Eva

Demian's mother, also a product of "magical thinking." Appropriately named, she functions as a symbol for Eve, the universal mother. As Demian is leading Sinclair toward his goal, it is Frau Eva who actually is his goal. She is Sinclair's fulfillment, at least in a symbolic sense.

Pistorius

A radical renegade theologian, who, in the absence of Demian aids Emil in his inward journey by teaching him about various religions, instructing him in the art of meditation, and interpreting the meaning of his dreams. When he can be of no more service to Sinclair, he is cast aside by the former student.

Franz Kromer

Young Sinclair's first link with the dark world, who, in effect, causes Sinclair to begin his quest for self-knowledge and the cementing of his friendship with Max Demian.

Knauer

A fellow student at Emil's boarding school who looks to him for advice. In a certain aspect, he is reminiscent of an earlier Sinclair, and, as such, illustrates Sinclair's development in the direction of Demian and Frau Eva.

Critical Commentaries

I. "TWO REALMS"

Demian begins through the narration of the main character, Emil Sinclair, concerning his youth as of 1904 or 1905. The entire novel depicts ten years' activity, which takes us up to his involvement as a German soldier in World War I, at which point Sinclair is twenty years old. It is important for the reader to keep in mind constantly that it is not the child Sinclair telling the story, but a mature adult reflecting back upon various stages of his development, trying to present an understandable analysis of what was occurring to him both internally and externally. Although it is obvious that the major key of the novel is *individual* and deals with the internal development of one character, the outcome presents a minor key which transcends the individual aspect to arrive at a universal meaning.

At the age of ten, young Emil Sinclair begins to become aware of a division in the world into light and dark, and good and evil. Critics have traced the source of Hesse's choice for his protagonist's name to Isaac von Sinclair, who was a friend of Holderlin. Others have pointed out, additionally, that the name is of further importance symbolically because it is an Anglo-French compound with the first syllable "sin" meaning dark, and the last syllable "clair" meaning light. Thus the awareness of a dichotomized world by a young boy who is going to come to grips with it and whose name represents it is an appropriate beginning for the novel.

To young Emil Sinclair, the world of light is epitomized by his home, his family, and their customs and traditions. The dark world borders and even overlaps his world with servant girls, ghost stories, and scandals. Young Sinclair can imagine the Devil lurking on a neighborhood corner, but can never recognize his presence within his household. The recognition and awe of the potential evils waiting on the outside makes Emil appreciative of the security and warmth of his home. In his self-perspective at this time, Sinclair identifies with the world of the righteous because he is the child of "saintly" parents. Recognizing the overlap, however, he is aware that he also lives in the darker world, although he is a stranger to it.

In viewing his ambition to become a part of the good and righteous world on his own part, he senses that he will have to journey through the dark world and its temptations in order to obtain success. Emil reflects upon stories he has heard of sons who have gone astray and who have eventually returned home into the fold with much happiness. A great deal of Hesse's writing deals to varying degrees with such themes as the Prodigal Son. In reading and hearing such stories, however, Sinclair is most fascinated with the parts dealing with the hero's involvement with evil. Hence, without consciously being aware of it, the young boy has sensed something about the forbidden, yet enticing, aspects of evil.

As the son of a rather prosperous family, Sinclair attends the elite Latin school, but it is his involvement with a public school student, the drunken tailor's son, Franz Kromer, that is the beginning of Sinclair's journey.

In an attempt to impress the older ruffian, Kromer, with his bravado, Sinclair invents a lie about his heroic part in the theft of some apples, and thus he makes himself susceptible to blackmail by Kromer. The imagined theft of "apples" is what ultimately leads to his downfall, and his exclusion from the "garden." Sinclair frequently refers to the domain of his parents by this term. Hence, very early in the narrative, Hesse employed a biblical allusion and set a religious tenor for the novel. Both the symbolism and tone will remain quite religious throughout the remainder of the novel. This aspect of the book is one of the devices employed by Hesse to build tension, because when contrasted with the Nietzschean philosophy expressed, seemingly irreconcilable paradoxes result. The addition of the psychological aspect to the religious and Nietzschean aspects further complicates the novel. Indeed, the psychological factor leads into areas considered taboo by much of society. These factors have caused at least one of Hesse's critics to avoid discussing *Demian* because he feels such discussion might cause too much controversy. This, however, is not the case if the novel is analyzed logically and carefully.

Further description of the villainous young Kromer reveals that he has a habit of spitting through a space between his two front teeth which gives him a somewhat serpent-like aspect. Kromer's threat of exposure forces Emil into a more serious, and this time an actual, crime. In order to pay Kromer the amount of blackmail money which he demands, Emil steals, first, from his own piggy bank and, then, from wherever he can, especially when he finds money lying around the house.

Contemplating his plight, Sinclair feels that he has now made a covenant with Satan and that his life is ruined. Debating whether or not to confess his predicament to his father and take the resulting punishment, as he has at times in the past, Sinclair decides that he must solve this problem by himself. His deep guilt feelings effect a break in his family ties. Sinclair withdraws from the mainstream of family activity. Occasionally reprimanded by his father for trivial matters, Sinclair both transfers his father's anger to his greater wrong-doing, and at the same time feels a contempt toward his father because of his ignorance of Emil's real crime. This latter feeling, which is a new experience for Emil, is the beginning of his quest for independence.

Sinclair begins to feel like an outsider, something evil within his parent's realm of righteousness, certain that God's grace is no longer with him. Yet he is also intuitively aware that the end of his former life will lead to the beginning of a new one. Sinclair also realizes that in the process of rebirth he must also sever the cord binding him to his mother, an act which is much more difficult for him than leaving his father.

Because of his fear of meeting with Kromer, Sinclair frequently becomes conveniently ill and hides within the safe confines of his house.

When Sinclair does finally face Kromer, without the full payment required to buy his silence, Kromer continues his bullying tactics and, at times, even forces Emil to become his slave, performing menial tasks. From this point on, the terrifying shrillness of Kromer's whistle summons Sinclair to his evil master for further nameless tortures. When at home, Emil remains withdrawn from his parents and sisters, whom he cannot imagine guilty of any type of wrongdoing. It is emphasized that his alienation is strongest toward his father, to whom he is completely cold. By the conclusion of the first chapter, Emil Sinclair has been forced to leave the "garden" of his childhood innocence and to venture precariously into the realm of the dark world.

II. "CAIN"

At the beginning of the second chapter, Emil informs the reader that his "salvation" came from an entirely unexpected source. The key word here is "salvation." A new student, Max Demian, who is several years older than Sinclair, has enrolled at the Latin school. Demian is obviously an outsider. He is different from everyone else of Emil's acquaintance. The unexplained aura about him isolates him from the other students. Though not popular, Demian is respected by the students because of his great self-assurance, especially toward his teachers.

While walking home from school one day, Sinclair is joined by Demian, who engages the reluctant younger boy in conversation. Demian makes a reference to a weathered escutcheon above the doorway of the Sinclair residence. Emil himself is vaguely aware of its existence, although he has never really looked at it. Demian identifies the carving as a sparrow hawk, thus establishing the central symbol of the story.

Demian also makes reference to a lesson which his class has shared with Sinclair's, the subject of which was the story of Cain and Abel. Demian provides his own interpretation of Cain and his mark. Sensing that the awarding of a special mark for an act of cowardice, a mark that protects Cain and puts the fear of God into others, is somewhat illogical, Demian states that Cain is a different and superior human being. Because Cain is "different" people are in awe of him and are suspicious and afraid of him. Rather than admit their own inferiority, these people invent stories about Cain and his people. Demian believes that Cain is guilty of murder, but does not pass a moral judgment against his action. In short, Demian's view of Cain emphasizes his nobility.

It is obvious in this discussion that the essence of Demian's commentary about Cain can also be applied to Demian himself. Demian's full name—Max Demian—provides insight into his character. "Max" could well be a shortened form of "maximus" meaning superlative. Demian is a name which came to Hesse in a dream and can be linked to his function in the novel as Sinclair's *daemon*. Among ancient peoples, a *daemon* was a spirit presiding over persons, places, and secret intentions. Ancient philosophers believed that each person had two *daemons*— one good and one evil. The term is frequently used in the writings of Carl Gustav Jung, whose influence on Hesse has already been mentioned.

The concept of the superiority of certain individuals, which Max has applied to the story of Cain, emphasizes the profound influence of the early existential philosopher Friedrich Nietzsche upon Hesse. In fact, Demian seems to be an enigmatic character because his structural aspect in the story, which is decidely religious, and his functional aspect, which is Nietzschean, seem to clash. This however, is not so and will be discussed later.

Demian's discussion of Cain greatly upsets Sinclair since it undercuts the pillar of his fundamental religious beliefs which he has never before questioned. Though Emil is disconcerted with the ideas stated by Demian, he is nevertheless pleased by Demian's manner and his aura of self-confidence manifested in his voice and especially through his eyes.

Reflecting back on the time when he was chastised by his father for his muddy boots and his secret feelings of superiority,

Emil recognizes his feelings as identifiable with Demian's interpretation of Cain. This realization and further thoughts of Demian's conversation forms the awakening of Emil's critical mind and his departure from a blind acceptance which is often said to be characteristic of childhood. For a time, at least, Emil has been so involved in thinking that he has forgotten about his predicament with Franz Kromer. Sinclair has begun to become involved in *living* and *thinking* about the total world in which he lives, encompassing both the light and the dark aspects of the dichotomized world of traditional Christianity.

Emil, however, has not been the only person to note the special qualities of Demian. Rumors are rampant. Some reports claim that the wealthy Demian is a Jew, or possibly Mohammedan. Later rumors will claim that he is an atheist, knows girls intimately, and is his mother's lover. One rumor concerning his physical prowess is confirmed when he humiliates and temporarily paralyzes the strongest boy in his class by a seemingly magical touch, probably directed at a vulnerable nerve. Thus to his less knowledgable contemporaries, Demian seems even more than unusual. He is almost god-like or demon-like.

Sinclair's short-lived escape from Kromer ends. But even in his dreams, he is tormented by Kromer. One dream initiates an Oedipus theme. Emil dreams that Kromer has forced him to wait in ambush, armed with a knife, for a certain person to pass by and this person always turns out to be his own father. However, Demian is also a subject of Emil's dreams and even takes Kromer's place as a torturer in two dreams.

The significance of the increased mention of dreams and dream-like states cannot be overstressed. As the story progresses, it becomes increasingly difficult to differentiate between what is reality and what is not reality because of Sinclair's constant dreaming. Ultimately, the question of the reality of Demian himself, as well as his mother arises. This problem will be discussed later.

Demian's next involvement in the story occurs while Kromer is once again terrorizing Sinclair, this time under Demian's analytical eyes. After Kromer's departure, it is only a matter of minutes and a few words until Demian is able to ascertain the reason for Emil's fear of Kromer. Emil is both repelled and fascinated by Demian's apparent psychic power. At this point, Sinclair notes that Demian seems to know him and understand him better than he does himself. He further adds that when Demian speaks, it is almost as though his own inner voice is conversing with him. Demian offers his assistance to Sinclair and tells him that he must free himself of Kromer's bondage if he wishes to have a meaningful life. Characteristically, Demian suggests that the most efficient method of achieving this would simply be to *kill* Kromer.

Approximately a week passes, during which time Sinclair has not once been bothered by Kromer's whistle. When Emil accidentally meets him on the street, Kromer turns aside to avoid facing Sinclair. Demian then admits that he has persuaded Kromer that it is in his best interest to stop plaguing Sinclair. He does not divulge his methodology, although he does say that he did not either pay Emil's debt or physically abuse Kromer. Emil remains perplexed.

His immediate problem and his necessary contact with the dark world at an end, Sinclair deserts his benefactor and returns to the womb—that is, back to his mother and the world of goodness; back to his lost paradise. The prodigal son has returned. The need now gone, Sinclair even confesses the whole episode to his parents and is subsequently forgiven and taken back into the fold. Sinclair, however, remains cognizant of the fact that things still are not and never will be as they once were. He also senses that Demian somehow, as well as Kromer, is a link to the dark world, although a different type of link.

Still dependent, still needing someone for support, Sinclair has returned to his parents. But he feels that possibly his confession, explanation, and gratitude should have been directed instead to Demian. His fear of Demian's encouragement toward independence has prevented him from seeking further contact. Demian's influence remains, nevertheless. A half year later, while walking with his father, he mentions Demian's interpretation of the Cain story. His father expounds upon it as a form of heresy and warns Sinclair about the dangers of entertaining such dangerous notions.

III. "AMONG THIEVES"

The title of the third chapter is once again a biblical allusion, which, once again, Demian will treat as a myth and interpret as he pleases. In this recurring practice, Demian reflects Hesse's own views. Hesse, as he stated in 1930, believed that biblical myths were useless unless they could be interpreted personally for the individual in his own time.

At this point, young Sinclair is just beginning to awaken sexually and is undergoing the agony of adolescence in coming to terms with those thoughts and desires deemed forbidden by society. As with most people at this point in their lives, Sinclair makes a further withdrawal from his family. Sinclair observes that leaving childhood and developing into adulthood is, for many people, the only time in their lives that they experience dying and rebirth, hinting that this should be a continual process if the individual is to attain the highest degree of fulfillment. Most individuals stop evolving, cling to their pasts, and dream of a lost state of innocence. It is implied that only superior beings — such as Demian — continue to evolve and seek their destiny. Again, obvious Nietzschean influence is observable.

While Franz Kromer has vanished from Sinclair's life, Demian will, from this point on, always be a part of his life. Reflecting back upon occasions when he has carefully observed Demian's uniqueness, Sinclair presents the first detailed physical description of his mentor.

Demian is described as having an ethereal appearance. His face contains characteristics of manliness, boyishness, and femininity. It is old looking, young looking and still ageless. He is handsome yet different. Sinclair observes that trees or animals could look this way but not people. Demian is extremely different from other people.

Several years pass before Sinclair again has close contact with Demian. Emil, now about fourteen years old, finds himself in the same confirmation class as Demian. Once again the lesson being taught is about Cain and Abel. Influenced by a fleeting glance from Demian, Sinclair this time is critical of the traditional interpretation given by the pastor. Soon Demian manages to move closer to Sinclair until he is sitting beside him. He accomplishes this feat even though the students have been alphabetically arranged by the pastor. The new bond established between the two boys enables Sinclair to fully understand just how remarkably different Demian is. He appears to control others with his thoughts. Even the pastor is subject to Demian's will, which he mysteriously manifests through his eyes. Demian also explains to Emil that his thought-reading and predictions of the actions of others are simply the product of intense observation.

Using the example of the night moth, Demian refutes the pastor's claim of free will. According to Demian, our will is free and we can obtain a particular goal only if the goal we have set is right and necessary to our individual needs and development. If the goal meets these criteria, we are capable of its attainment. Demian explains that he was able to accomplish changing his seat even though the pastor's will was in opposition to his by utilization of this principle.

Further development of Sinclair's independence is effected by Demian through the biblical account of Golgotha. Demian admires the unrepentant thief as a man of character and strength. The thief had been evil all his life and chose not to repent, but rather to follow his destiny in accord with the way he had lived. Demian believes that this thief might even have been a descendant of Cain, and labels the other thief a "sniveling convert."

At this time it is advisable to reflect upon all of Demian's characteristics as described up to this point. The first reference to him was in the words of Sinclair: "my salvation." Indeed, Demian did save Emil from the serpent-like Kromer, after Sinclair had caused his own expulsion from the "garden." Demian also seems to be almost magical, performing such "miracles" as thought reading and displaying uncanny knowledge of others, both physically and mentally. Subject of much suspicion, Demian is an unusual outsider who is, however, held in respect. He instructs Sinclair through parables and disputes things with his teachers. His difference is made even more apparent because of the unexplained aura which surrounds him. Later he will, in a sense, have a band of disciples. His physiognomy is, at the same time, masculine and feminine, possibly displaying the sensitive gentility frequently present in portraits of Christ. Even the chapter title could also refer as well as to Demian, who (figuratively) has been placed between two thieves, namely Sinclair and Kromer. There can be no doubt that Demian has been established as, and functions as, a Christ figure.

Yet, paradoxically, the essence of his words has been anything but Christ-like. Ironically, Demian is the mouthpiece for the "superman" doctrines of Nietzsche. To Hesse, this is not at all incongruous, as will be demonstrated later.

Demian's next attack on orthodox Christianity hits Sinclair harder and more personally than any of his previous tirades. Demian sees a serious weakness in any religion which arbitrarily sets up an attitude of attributing all that is good to God and all that is evil to Satan, when, in effect, God created the entire world and therefore deserves total responsibility. To make his argument more persuasive to Emil, Demian refers to God as the father of all life, and then to the religious and societal repression of all sexual matters. The clergy frequently refers to such matters as being the work of the devil. Demian's suggestion is that *all* of life should be affirmed and the arbitrary, illogical, and artificial dichotomy dispensed with.

Sinclair is now suddenly aware that his secret agony concerning the dark and light worlds is not uniquely his, as he previously thought, but rather a problem common to all mankind. Demian also informs Sinclair that now that he has begun to think critically, he will no longer be able to repress all of his darker urgings. Frustrated by all of this sudden illumination, Sinclair becomes defiant, asserting his belief that merely because evil exists as a fact of life, one cannot justify participation in it. Demian's concluding Nietzschean response is that Sinclair must realize the relativity of morality, citing the ancient Greek celebration of sexuality as a contrast to the Christian repression of it. Therefore, it is for each person to decide for himself what is permitted and forbidden for *him*, and then to stand by his own beliefs. It is possible here to observe some influence of Dostoevsky. Hesse was very familiar with his works, and this train of thought parallels Raskolnikov's thoughts in *Crime and Punishment*.

Sinclair's next reminiscence of Demian is again set in their confirmation class. Gazing at Demian, he observes his friend in a trance-like state resembling death, his face like a mask of stone. Demian is obviously deep within himself in the process of meditation. Meditation is a recurrent step in the search for self in all of Hesse's subsequent novels from *Siddhartha* to *The Glass Bead Game (Magister Ludi)*. Shortly after this scene, Sinclair makes unsuccessful attempts at emulating Demian. Meditation remains an art which Sinclair will need to master on his journey to his own interior.

Emil's childhood is now gone and his confirmation completed. It is determined that following his vacation he will be sent away from home to further his education at a boarding school. He soon finds himself alone, in a strange situation, in a strange town, without the crutches of his family, with whom he has long been severing ties, and without Demian.

IV. "BEATRICE"

At the boarding school, Sinclair soon finds himself an outsider, as Demian was previously viewed at the Latin school. He is at first neither liked nor respected by his classmates. His adolescent awkwardness has even caused him to dislike himself. Agonizingly alone, Sinclair soon finds the road to his much needed acceptance through a friendship with Alfons Beck, the oldest boy in his boarding house. Under Beck's tutelage, Sinclair once again finds himself immersed in a dark world. He begins to frequent bars and to associate with the disorderly crowd. Rebelling against all forms of authority, he is soon in academic difficulties. His reaction to this and to everything that happens to him, even his father's admonitions, is indifference. Despite his resultant feeling of self-hatred, Sinclair revels in his degradation, enjoying a new-found reputation of being an impressive character in this world of debauchery. The only significant difference between Sinclair and his comrades is that Emil maintains his sexual innocence. Yet with his loneliness terribly acute and his expulsion from school a near certainty, Sinclair finally finds his way back to himself.

His salvation this time is self-effected. During a spring walk in a park, Sinclair observes an attractive young girl whom he names Beatrice, after Dante's first love. Although Emil never meets or talks to the young lady, he sets her upon a pedestal and worships her from afar. Beatrice is described as being tall, slender, and boyish looking. Sometimes when added to past discussions, such as Demian's feminine aspect and Sinclair's sexual innocence, young readers think that his attraction to a boyish looking girl is indicative of a latent homosexual trait. Here again, the explanation and understanding must be sought in Jung's influence on Hesse.

Jung believed that no human being was entirely masculine or feminine, but rather that all humans possess characteristics of each sex in varying degrees. The female aspect in a man's personality was labelled the *anima* by Jung. Correspondingly, each woman has an *animus* which is her masculine aspect. The *anima* consists of such traits as the irrational, the sensual, the intuitive, and the sensitive, which Western men have been forced to repress by society in order to develop such traits such as the mechanical, the logical, the practical, and the rational.

These repressed aspects of the male, however, are not totally benign. They simmer beneath the surface somewhere in the collective unconscious, and they manifest themselves by influencing the conscious ego. Hence, a man, intuitively aware of his peculiar female aspect, sometimes projects it upon actual women, recognizing in an actual woman characteristics complementary to himself. Beatrice can therefore be considered Sinclair's *anima.*

The second Jungian archetype concerning the collective unconscious is the self. The self is an inner voice, which frequently manifests itself in the form of dreams which speak to and influence the conscious ego. In dream form, it usually appears as a person of the same sex as the dreamer, although it can appear as an animal or even a hermaphroditic figure. Recalling Sinclair's earlier description of Demian as combining both masculine and feminine features, or even his observation that "animals could look like that," it becomes apparent that Demian represents Sinclair's self. Thus only through the synthesis of Sinclair, Demian, and Beatrice can Sinclair be complete or fulfilled.

Sinclair realizes that in his state of degradation he is not worthy of Beatrice and he decides to repent of his evil ways. Consciously correcting his bad habits, he soon solves his academic difficulties and begins to enjoy better acceptance by the other students.

Still plagued by loneliness, because he lacks a real friend, he finds it necessary to create new ways of occupying his time. Inspired by Beatrice, he decides to paint. His first conscious attempts to reproduce her face fail. Sinclair then gives way to his imagination and allows his brush to flow at will. In this way the *anima* aspect of his unconscious manifests itself. It might be added that artistry, or creativity in an aesthetic sense such as painting is, of course, one of those characteristics considered to be largely feminine. Sinclair himself emphasizes the "dreaming" aspect of his painting activity, and likens its product to the manifestation of his subconscious mind. Finally, one day a

face which intrigues Sinclair is completed. The painted counte-
nance is stiff and masklike, half masculine, half feminine, and
yet somehow ageless. Awakening from a dream one morning,
Sinclair imagines that the face seems to know him, like a mother,
and calls to him. Emil, staring at the strange brightness of the
forehead and the expression of the eyes, recognizes the portrait
as being that of Demian. Pinning the painting to his window and
allowing the sunlight to shine through it, Emil further senses
that the painting is not actually of Beatrice or Demian, but
rather it is a reflection of himself, his inner self, his *daemon,*
symbolizing the essence of his whole future life.

Once again it should be emphasized that all of this activity
occurs in a dream-like state. Whether or not he actually ever pins
the portrait to the window could be debated.

Thinking of his sorely missed friend, Emil reflects back
upon their last meeting during one of his school vacations. Over
a glass of wine, the two boys are discussing Emil's school life
and his then existent period of rebellion. Demian appears to
accept but frown upon Emil's drinking habits, but adds that
sometimes a life of hedonism can be a type of preparation for
sainthood. He cites St. Augustine as an example of this principle.
As a final consolation to Sinclair, Demian adds that we are all
fortunate because within us there is someone who knows all
and wills all. This is an obvious reference to the subconscious;
Emil, through Demian's carefully selected words, identifies with
St. Augustine's example and realizes that this is the direction in
which his life has gone.

On the night of the flashback, Sinclair has a terrifying dream.
He remembers the coat of arms above the doorway to his house
and dreams that Demian forces him to swallow it. He feels
the heraldic bird coming to life within him. The bird then begins
to eat away from within. Horrified, he awakens from the dream.

Once again, the central symbol of the novel becomes important. Remembering his dream, Sinclair decides to paint a
picture of the heraldic bird. It should be remembered and noted,

however, that as he himself previously stated, Sinclair has never really looked carefully at the details of the coat of arms, which are not readily observable anyway because it has been obscured by age and many coats of paint.

When the painting is completed, it is of a sparrow hawk with half its body enclosed in a dark globe from which it is struggling to free itself, as if hatching from an egg. The fact that the bird is identifiable as a sparrow hawk indicates that it is a grown bird, not a chick. The picture therefore is representative not of birth but of rebirth. The question arises as to why the painting took this specific form when Sinclair did not really know what the coat of arms looked like specifically. The answer concerning this most important symbol of the novel is again to be found in the influence of Jung, filtered to Hesse by his many psychoanalytic sessions with Joseph B. Lang.

Hesse has emphasized the dream aspect of the painting. The dream-like state has also been connected to the subconscious. The term "subconscious" is a Freudian term, replaced with "unconscious" by Jung, who felt the prefix "sub" to be demeaning to what he felt was a higher form of innate awareness. According to Jung, the human mind contains two aspects of the unconscious. The first and most obvious consists of memories of actual events which have happened to the individual and have been either forgotten or repressed. The second, and, in this case, the most important aspect of the unconscious, he termed the "collective unconscious." This concept is absolutely necessary in the discussion of *Demian*, as well as all of Hesse's later novels.

The "collective unconscious" does not consist of memories specific to the individual, but rather consists of intuitive knowledge concerning universal human experiences, passed along in the species during the evolutionary process. In other words, there are certain symbols which convey similar intuitive meanings to all people. Such a symbol is called an "archetype." The egg (the dark globe of Sinclair's sparrow hawk painting) is such a symbol; it can be traced back to ancient Roman times when, according to the late anthropologist Bachofen, it represented the two poles of the world. Thus the sparrow hawk, breaking out of the egg, to be reborn, is shattering the world of unreal, arbitrary, and false polarities—much as Sinclair himself is trying to do. Hence, the symbol is an internal one for Sinclair at this point, although at the end of the novel it will be external and universal.

In a "dream-like" state, Sinclair mails this painting to Demian although he does not know his present whereabouts. To the painting Sinclair adds no message at all, not even his name.

V. "THE BIRD FIGHTS ITS WAY OUT OF THE EGG"

One day, shortly after mailing the painting, during a break between classes, Sinclair notices a note tucked into one of his books. Recognizing that the note is folded in a special manner peculiar to his classmates, he does not immediately open it. During his next lesson, while obviously "daydreaming," Sinclair opens the note. He is struck dumb by its message: "The bird fights its way out of the egg. The egg is the world. Who would be born must first destroy a world. The bird flies to God. That God's name is Abraxas." Sinclair interprets the note as being Demian's response to his gift of the painting. A logical question now arises. How did Demian get the note into Sinclair's book, and even if he did, how did he know how to fold it in the special manner of Sinclair's classmates? The answer can be approached in two different ways which provide insight on two different levels.

As the chapter progresses, Sinclair is startled out of his reverie (caused by the note) when his teacher mentions the name Abraxas during a lecture on Herodotus. Abraxas is the name of an ancient Gnostic deity. It is not, however, referred to in the writings of Herodotus. The young teacher, Dr. Follens, has just completed his university training. It has been mentioned previously in the novel that Demian is somewhere attending a university. Perhaps the young instructor is the messenger who delivered the message. Possibly he has had some contact with Demian. If such contact has occurred it could explain the oddity of the messages of the note and the corresponding lecture.

Another way of viewing this strange episode is to reflect upon the past emphasis on the "dream" aspect or potential unreality of some of the previous events. Possibly, this whole sequence of events took place only in Sinclair's mind. Maybe he actually wrote the note himself in one of his dream-like moments or maybe it didn't even exist outside of his dream world. This becomes the noticeable beginning of a sequence of events when Demian (self) and, later, his mother *(anima)* become increasingly internalized within Sinclair, thus indicating Sinclair's process of attaining a harmony of his various parts. This has been hinted at from the beginning when, in his amazement at Demian's ability to see inside others, Emil stated that it was as if Demian knew more about him than he himself. Perhaps, then, Demian is, or has become, Emil's own unconscious. Hesse himself offered a comment about trying to rationally analyze the characters of Demian and Frau Eva when he stated that they were figures "that encompass and signify far more than is accessible to rational consideration; they are magical conjurations."

Abraxas becomes the second important symbol of this novel. Abraxas is Demian's answer to the previously stated problem of a God who represents an arbitrarily selected half of the world. Abraxas is a deity who serves to unite the entire world, the light and the dark, the godly and the devilish. He does not represent either; rather, he is the affirmation of both.

Sinclair experiences an intensification of his sexual drive. His longing for meaningful love seems hopeless. Sinclair again retreats into his dream world, which has become as active during his waking hours as during his sleep. A new dream occurs which he explicitly and emphatically identifies as the most significant dream of his life.

In this dream Sinclair is entering his father's house beneath the heraldic hawk on the escutcheon. His mother is walking toward him with outstretched arms. As they are about to embrace, she suddenly changes. She now resembles Demian, or, more accurately, Emil's portrait. Sinclair is taken, enveloped in a passionate embrace which leaves him with feelings of both ecstacy and horror. He sees the embrace as both a crime and an act of worship. Utterly confused, he awakens, sometimes elated, sometimes guilt ridden. Here the motif of incest is clearly presented. One of the strongest taboos of every human society has been touched upon. It should be pointed out, however, that the dream is not of actual incest. Later, it will become more clear that the female figure is not Sinclair's mother, but, rather, is Demian.

Jung, in discussing the sun myth, which can be related to the Gnostic god Abraxas, explains that the basis of incestuous desire lies in the wish to become a child once more, to return to the protective womb of the mother for rebirth. This, however, is forbidden because the mother's body would have to be entered in order for the impregnation necessary for the reproduction of oneself to occur. The rebirth myths invent various substitutes for the mother in order to prevent the libido from sinking to actual incest. Hesse will, therefore, replace and make clear that the figure in question is Demian's mother and that the desire shown in the dream is symbolic rather than actual. Frau Eva will represent various things but mostly what her name indicates, the concept of a universal mother.

Sinclair is now near the end of high school and is soon to enter the university. Despite his adequacy as a student, however, he is still plagued by a lack of direction. His only goal is to come to terms with himself. Through his narration, it is obvious that despite his sense of futility, he has progressed a great deal. Emil actually now possesses some of the traits peculiar to Demian when he was first introduced to him. Sinclair also can intuitively analyze people and occasionally startles his fellow students with his mystical skills.

Still in the habit of taking evening walks to pass the time, Sinclair is attracted one night to a small church by the sound of some rather unorthodox organ music. After listening outside for a number of nights, he finally gains enough courage to follow the organist to a tavern. During the conversation with the organist, Pistorius, Sinclair states that the quality he admires most about his music is its amorality: it combines both heaven and hell and he associates it with Abraxas, whose name he mentions.

Pistorius, the son of a respected clergyman, and a renegade theologian himself, is shocked by Sinclair's mention of Abraxas and is further drawn to Emil. Pistorius is also familiar with Abraxas; in fact, he knows a great deal about him, which he promises to discuss with Sinclair at a later time. During the course of an evening at the house of the organist's father, Pistorius explains his interest in studying all religions and his fascination concerning what sorts of gods people have created. His viewpoint of religion as mythology is what has made it inappropriate for him to serve as a clergyman. It is here in his room, before the fireplace, that Pistorius teaches Sinclair the art of meditation.

At their next meeting, Pistorius assumes his role as a psychologist, again utilizing Jung's concept of the collective unconscious. Many critics have stated that Hesse is actually portraying his own period of psychoanalysis and that Pistorius represents, in actuality, Dr. J. B. Lang. Pistorius teaches Sinclair that all human possibilities and potentialities are contained within each one of us. Sinclair's reaction to this is to question. If all things are complete within us, why do we keep striving? The answer Pistorius provides is that most people are simply unaware that his completeness and potential exists. It is this very awareness that should be sought after.

The psychological skills of Pistorius also include the interpreting of dreams. Sinclair's dream of fear, at finding himself able to fly, is interpreted by Pistorius. The ability to fly in dreams is common to many people. Its source is our own innate awareness of our power. However, most people are afraid to recognize their own potential and thus they refuse to fly. The earth offers more security. Others become too exhilarated with the free feeling and soar off into infinity and are subsequently labeled insane.

Still others, like Demian and Sinclair, become aware of their power and develop means to harness it and use it effectively. The means of control, however, is not invented; it comes from within. Pistorius concludes with an analogy of certain types of fish which possess a type of air bladder which can function as a type of lung left, a relic ages ago, still remaining after thousands of years of evolution.

VI. "JACOB WRESTLING"

At the onset of chapter six, Emil Sinclair is a young man of eighteen. Because of the teachings of Pistorius, he has learned a great deal about self-acceptance and self-reliance, as well as about human nature in a more universal sense. With Pistorius, Sinclair has been very open, sharing his inner feelings and dreams. There is one exception, though. Sinclair has never told Pistorius about his one dark dream, the haunting dream of his return home and of the forbidden embrace of the half-masculine, half-motherly figure.

Pistorius continues to encourage Sinclair to listen to his dreams, to seek after them, and above all, not to fear them. Much earlier Demian had told Sinclair that he had to learn what was permitted and what was forbidden for him individually. This brought up the concept of individual morality, and Emil's statement that evil acts are not justified simply because they exist. Sinclair questioned whether a wrong such as murder could be justified. Demian did not provide a definite answer at that time, saying only that Sinclair had to sense and do what he thought he should do. Pistorius and Sinclair also touch upon this concept. This time, however, it is discussed from a psychological point-of-view, rather than as a purely philosophical concept. Concerning the justification of murder, Pistorius claims that, at times, it could be permissible although most often not. He tells Sinclair that he must discern whether or not such urges are simply Abraxas interacting with the individual. His rationale is that if an individual hates another so much that he wants to kill him, it is usually because there is some specific characteristic in the other person that he hates. Pistorius adds that the hatred is directed toward that specific aspect which is also present in the person himself. What is not part of ourselves doesn't bother us. Therefore murder would be a mistake. Again though, Pistorius stresses that all of reality is relative to the individual.

During his final term in high school, Sinclair is suddenly approached one day by a younger student named Knauer. Knauer has been carefully observing Sinclair and is aware of his unique qualities, his "mark of Cain." It is Knauer's desire to befriend Sinclair and to learn whatever Sinclair can teach him, while he himself offers some interesting concepts to Emil. Knauer knows a bit about the mystical world and such things as white magic. Knauer's deepest problem is his fear of his own sexuality. He expresses his belief that continence is necessary for spiritual purity. Sinclair disagrees with this idea. Although he has never had any sort of sexual contact with a woman, he feels that he should and would have sex under the proper conditions, namely mutual love. Sinclair informs Knauer that he can tell him nothing; he must find his own way by listening to his inner voice. Disappointed and disillusioned, young Knauer leaves in a fit of anger after insulting Sinclair.

After painting another picture, once again in a dream-like state, of his dark dream image, Sinclair begins to worship it. The words of the biblical Jacob exhorting the blessing of the angel he has wrestled into submission come to Emil's mind. This partly explains the significance of the chapter title. Emil is clinging to the figure he has imprisoned on canvas, and is asking its blessing. During this particular trance Sinclair's mind flashes to the remote past, even pre-existence, and then to the future.

Waking from his deep sleep, he finds the painting mysteriously missing. He is unable to remember what happened to it, but thinks he might have burned it, and that possibly in his dream he burned it in his palm, and then ate the ashes. The most probable answer is that the painting existed only in Sinclair's mind.

Restless, Sinclair ventures into the night and finds himself hurriedly drawn through the town by some unidentifiable force until he arrives at a new, partially constructed building. The setting is reminiscent of Sinclair's earlier liaison with Kromer. Here, inside the building, he finds the student Knauer, cowering in the dark, waiting for daybreak to implement his plan of suicide. Sinclair has saved Knauer's life. There is no rational explanation for this event. However, keeping in mind the chapter title, the occurrence seems fitting because Jacob also saved a life through his struggle with the angel. Once again Sinclair's progression, both inward and upward, is apparent through this scene, which is comparable to Demian's earlier salvation of Emil.

In the subsequent conversations with Pistorius, Sinclair learns a great deal more about religions. He learns about Abraxas, reads from the Vedas, and even speaks the sacred "Om." Shortly, however, Sinclair realizes that he has absorbed all the knowledge that Pistorius has to offer. Knowledge is communicable but wisdom is not. Pistorius has been of great value in presenting knowledge, but when one considers Pistorius's utilizing or living all that he endorses, Pistorius is a failure. Unable to resist a sudden impulse caused by a moment of frustration, Sinclair blurts out this opinion to Pistorius, deeply wounding him and causing a breach between the two which will never really heal. Despite his immediate guilt feelings, Sinclair is unable to apologize because he feels the fundamental truth of what he had said. Thus, the student has surpassed his teacher.

Sinclair comes to believe that each individual has but one real function in life: he must find the way to himself. What his vocation might turn out to be, whether the person turns out good or evil is of no real consequence. The important concern is simply for the individual to seek his own destiny. Any other approach to life leads to shallowness and unfulfillment.

VII. "EVA"

During vacation, prior to entering the university, Sinclair travels to Demian's former residence in his home town to inquire as to his whereabouts. The old woman now living there shows Sinclair a photograph of Demian's mother. It is here that he realizes that this is the woman of his disturbing dream; she is his *daemon* and she does exist.

Encouraged by this realization, Sinclair begins to look for her everywhere. Shortly after this event, in the university town, Sinclair once again, seemingly by accident, meets Demian, who informs Sinclair that the meeting was anticipated and that the initially attracting "mark of Cain" is now much more prominent on Emil's forehead. While talking about their respective pasts, the conversation is suddenly shifted to the state of affairs in Europe. Demian speaks of the inward rottenness of the various European societies and maintains that their collapse is inevitable. Once again Demian functions as a Nietzschean mouthpiece. The "herd instinct" of the fearful masses is condemned, and the shallow meaninglessness of the Europeans' lives is emphasized. Demian senses that Europe will collapse and then be reborn. The year is now 1913 and what he actually senses is the fast approaching holocaust of World War I.

It is at this point that the larger and most important aspect of the story becomes externalized. Throughout the novel, Sinclair and Demian have been compulsively concerned with themselves. Possibly they have been viewed as very egocentric. But it is only now that the several apparent paradoxes can be resolved. Demian now reveals the purpose of those with the "mark of Cain" when he visualizes the aftermath of the forthcoming chaos. It will revolve around those with the "mark," those who will determine the future. After the war, there will be no more oppression of the individual will and the further development of the human species will once again be possible. Demian states that this goal, the ultimate perfection of the human race, is one expressed by both Jesus and Nietzsche. Now it is clear that Hesse has made a parallel in these two diverse doctrines, and the fact that the Christ figure, Demian, speaks the existential doctrine of Nietzsche is no longer a problem once it is clear that their respective goals are the same. Nietzsche had implored the isolated individuals, who were a chosen people, to seek solitude and self-understanding in order to bene-fit many others later. Thus Hesse's emphasis on self-knowledge is not really selfish in nature. Through a thorough understanding of self, one becomes more able to serve. Indeed, this idea of service is contained even more obviously in Hesse's other works: *Siddhartha, Narcissus and Goldmund, The Journey to the East,* and *The Glass Bead Game (Magister Ludi).*

The next day Emil's dream becomes reality. He finally meets Demian's mother, Frau Eva, in the hallway of their home beneath his sparrow hawk painting. Momentarily speechless, Sinclair takes Frau Eva's hands, kisses them, and finally feels fulfillment. When Sinclair announces that his whole life has been a journey toward this goal and he has now reached home, Frau Eva smiles at him like a "mother." The first description of Frau Eva stresses the same characteristics possessed by Demian, only magnified infinitely.

During his first conversation with Frau Eva, she stresses to Sinclair that dreams must be followed until realized, but that each dream is replaced by another.

Emil's reaction to the meeting and to Frau Eva is mani-fold. He is totally in awe of her, worships her, and yet, as sug-gested in his dream, he also loves her in a physical sense and desires her. Through Frau Eva, he comes to realize that his quest for awareness and harmony is different from the goals of the masses because the masses seek to preserve humanity as it was, while those with the "mark of Cain" sought an unknown distant goal for humanity which transcended the human condition at present.

The Demian residence serves as a meeting place for many types of intellectuals and philosophers, varying from astrologers to Buddhists to a disciple of Tolstoy. Those with the "mark of Cain" remained still somewhat isolated, forming an inner circle, concentrating on achieving such a level of awareness that no matter what would happen to the world, they would be able to understand it, remain stable, and if called upon to do so, to lead.

Demian speaks about the soul of Europe and in doing so is very reminiscent of Hesse himself in *Blick in Chaos*. In his essay on *The Brothers Karamazov*, he refers to the concept of a new breed of "Russian man." This peculiar being is a type of amoral beast not subject to any existing laws, combining the ferocity of an animal with the gentility of a saint, the splendor of God and the horror of Satan. Those with the "mark" must be ready.

Paralleling an earlier sensation in the story concerning Demian, Sinclair notices that when Frau Eva is present at the conversations of the group, that all of his thinking seems to come from her and eventually to return to her. He gradually begins to sense that she seems, also, like a reflection of his inner being.

Sinclair's physical longing for Frau Eva grows in intensity. Sensitive to his feelings, Frau Eva guides Sinclair through stories. She feels that in order to find fulfillment in love, one must not consciously seek to be loved, but rather must learn to manifest his own love first. When a person becomes able to love, then the love of others, sensing this quality, will be attracted to that person.

One day in early spring, Sinclair, upon entering Max's room, observes him in a trance-like state resembling that which occurred during their confirmation class. Disturbed, he questions Frau Eva, who assures him that there is no need for alarm. Still upset, Sinclair goes for a walk. While walking in a gentle rain, he observes a strange phenomenon in the distant sky. Watching colliding cloud banks, he sees a gigantic bird emerge and take flight, causing thunderous sounds with its beating wings. The storm then becomes violent, mixed with hail, for a brief moment. It is followed by a sudden burst of sunlight and an unreal serenity. Once again, the symbolism of the sparrow hawk and the egg is employed. This time, however, the hawk is not just an internal symbol for Sinclair's development, but it is external and universal, and it foreshadows the literal destruction of a world — that is, the destruction of pre-World War I Europe and the rebirth which is to follow. The bird becomes a harbinger of the war.

Sinclair describes his vision to Demian. Understanding Sinclair's vision, Demian associates it with a recent dream of his in which he visualized a vast, blazing landscape. Frau Eva also appears to have had a similar presentiment.

VIII. "THE END BEGINS"

Just prior to the end of the summer semester, after which Sinclair is scheduled to reluctantly return home, he is in his room, thinking about Frau Eva, willing her to come to him with as much psychic force as he can muster. Responding to the sudden sound of a horse in the street below, Sinclair descends to meet Demian, who announces the beginning of the war and his commission as a lieutenant. Demian also informs Sinclair that it was Frau Eva who sent him and that she sensed his call.

Sinclair has that evening's meal as Frau Eva's only guest. Just as he is about to leave, she informs him that whenever he needs her, all he need to do is appeal to her in the same manner as he had that day.

The following winter finds Sinclair on the front lines. As a participant in the war, he senses that the horrible fighting and death that he observes all around him is merely a different type of sign for the same principle represented by his sparrow hawk. The manifested hatred is not in actuality directed toward the enemy, but is rather directed violently at the divided individual soul which must first be destroyed before it can be reborn.

One night while on guard duty in Belgium, Sinclair is gazing at the sky while braced against the trunk of a tree. The tree as a location for the occurrence of an enlightening experience becomes a strong motif in Hesse's writings from *Demian* on. In the clouds Sinclair visualizes a city, teeming with people. Suddenly there appears a godlike giant figure resembling Frau Eva. She swallows up the people, figuratively taking them back into the womb. In resultant agony, she falls to the ground, the "mark" bright on her forehead. As she utters a terrifying scream, thousands of stars spring from her forehead. One of these stars, actually a piece of shrapnel from an explosion, reaches Sinclair, seriously wounding him. Hesse's source for this scene is obviously the account of the Daughter of Zion in the Book of Revelations.

After a period of vague consciousness, Sinclair finds himself in a field hospital. Turning on his mattress, he notices that the mattress beside his is also occupied. It is Demian. Quietly making brief references to the past, even to the long, unmentioned Kromer episode, Demian calmly tells Sinclair that he will soon depart, but that the next time he is needed, all Emil need do is to listen within and he will find him. As a final gesture he gives Sinclair a kiss from Frau Eva.

Upon reawakening, Emil finds the neighboring cot occupied by a stranger. The transubstantiation complete, Sinclair has now internalized Demian. The synthesis is finished; Demian and Sinclair are one. The conscious ego (Sinclair) has merged with the self (Demian) and through Demian, with the *anima* (Frau Eva). At least to as great a degree as possible for Sinclair, harmony is achieved. In his last comment he states that dressing the wound hurt as has everything that has happened to him since. Sinclair has not attained the perfect rapture which he has sought, but he has had a taste of it. The answer to the pain of living, he has learned, now lies within him. He has achieved awareness and inner peace and can subsequently draw upon this when life places obstacles in his path.

It should be noted that the only Hesse hero to achieve complete, permanent fulfillment or a state of Nirvana is Siddhartha. In conclusion, it is important for the reader to remember Hesse's own statement about Demian and Frau Eva. While they certainly are real characters in the story, they also have a profound influence on Sinclair's mind, and at times necessarily seem like only parts of his mind. Their existence and activities cannot always be rationally explained, but they need not be; they are the products of Hesse's "magical thinking."

Character Analyses

EMIL SINCLAIR

The young protege of Demian is far from being an average person. Recognized by Max Demian as a possessor of the "mark" of uniqueness at the age of ten, Sinclair is guided by Demian and others in his search for complete cognition of what it is to be a human being and to subsequent fulfillment. Hesse, in his prologue, has told us that every individual is special. In each, nature is attempting to complete the human evolutionary process by creating the ultimate human. Sinclair follows the triadic development constantly utilized by Hesse. He falls from childhood innocence, suffers much of the anguish of life and finally, through his acute self-knowledge, transcends his despair to a state of semi-harmony with life and self. As all of Hesse's writing is autobiographical to varying degrees, Sinclair in describing his attitudes, sufferings, and search for self, can be considered the voice of the author himself.

MAX DEMIAN

Demian is a puzzling figure. He is obviously very important but only in terms of his relationship to Sinclair. Serving in the novel as a Christ-like figure who leads Sinclair in his quest, Demian is also the spokesman for the philosophical influence of Nietzsche upon Hesse. Demian seems at times like a real character with supernatural qualities. At other times he seems more like a figment of Sinclair's imagination or perhaps his subconscious rather than as a real person. He is probably somewhere in between. He does, however, serve as Sinclair's *daemon,* or inner voice, possibly only through his inspiration, which serves to activate the deeper recesses of Sinclair's mind. The reader should not be discouraged if he finds that Demian defies logical explanation. Hesse intended Demian to be this way.

FRAU EVA

Demian's mother's major function is related to her name. She represents the concept of the "universal mother." Possessing all the qualities of Demian, but in greater intensity, she comes to represent that very goal for which Sinclair is striving. She also frequently seems more like a part of Sinclair's subconscious than like an actual person. Subsequently she, like her son, defies rational explanation.

PISTORIUS

Pistorius is a character whom Sinclair meets while in high school and apart from Demian. He also serves as a guide for Sinclair, providing him with a vast background of religious knowledge, particularly about the Gnostic deity Abraxas. Serving also as an amateur psychologist, the character of Pistorius is probably based upon Dr. J. B. Lang, who aided Hesse during his period of mental strife. Pistorius is finally surpassed by his student and is cast aside because Sinclair must ultimately find his own way.

KNAUER

Knauer is a high school student a few years younger than Sinclair. His only important function in the story is as a device by which Sinclair's growth toward his goal can be illustrated. When Sinclair saves Knauer's life, Sinclair can be compared to an earlier Demian, who figuratively effected Emil's salvation.

FRANZ KROMER

Kromer is Sinclair's first human link with the dark world. When he blackmails the young Sinclair, he, in effect, begins Sinclair on his journey. His bullying tactics also serve to cement a friendship between Sinclair and Demian, who comes to his rescue.

Review Questions

1. Demonstrate how Demian's function as a Christ figure can be reconciled to his being a spokesman for Nietzsche's ideas.

2. Discuss whether or not Demian and Frau Eva are real characters or whether they exist only in Sinclair's mind.

3. Explain the terms "collective unconscious," "*anima*," and "archetype."

4. How does the heraldic bird function as a symbol for Sinclair and how does it eventually transcend its individual nature to become universal?

5. Discuss various aspects of Demian and Frau Eva which can be attributed to Hesse's concept of "magical thinking."

6. Demonstrate by specific references why the goal of those with the "mark" is not an egocentric one.

7. List various characteristics of Demian which identify him as a Christ figure.

8. In what ways do both Demian and Pistorius emphasize that morality is relative to the individual?

9. Discuss Sinclair as the "conscious ego," Demian as the "self," and Beatrice or Frau Eva as "*anima*."

10. Discuss the various biblical allusions and what function each one serves.

11. Show how Sinclair's life can be divided into three distinguishable periods.

12. Discuss the various stages of Sinclair's struggle for independence from his family.

13. Discuss the importance of the concept of human evolution as depicted in the novel.

Annotated Selected Bibliography

Baumer, Franz. *Hermann Hesse.* New York: Frederick Ungar Publishing Company, 1969. This translation of the German edition of 1959 is a useful and easily read short work dealing with the latter part of Hesse's life. It is more useful as a biographical piece than as a source of criticism of Hesse's works.

Boulby, Mark. *Hermann Hesse: His Mind and Art.* Ithaca, New York: Cornell University Press, 1968. This book, available only in hardback, is an exhaustive study of Hesse's works in all their aspects. Its coverage spans the entire literary life of Hesse and shows great objective insight.

Casebeer, Edwin F. *Hermann Hesse.* New York: Warner Books, Inc., 1972. This paperback edition concerns itself only with the works following *Demian.* It is, however, well written and extremely useful in its discussion of the psychological aspects of Hesse's later works.

Field, George Wallis. *Hermann Hesse.* New York: Twayne Publishers, Inc., 1970. This paperback is a comprehensive study of Hesse's entire literary life and is extremely useful for its biographical information, as well as for its criticism.

Fleissner, Else M. *Hermann Hesse: Modern German Poet and Writer.* Charlotteville, New York: Story House Corp., 1972. This short pamphlet is useful for a quick account of Hesse's life and the introduction of some of his major themes. It is also extremely easy to understand.

Freedman, Ralph. *The Lyrical Novel: Studies in Hermann Hesse, Andre Gide, and Virginia Woolf.* Princeton: Princeton University Press, 1963. This paperback approaches Hesse as a poetic writer who frequently bares his soul through the autobiographical aspects of his works. It treats especially Hesse's Romantic imagination and his use of allegory.

Mileck, Joseph. *Hermann Hesse and His Critics.* New York: AMS Press Inc., 1972. This hardback by one of the leading Hesse scholars is useful primarily because of its summations and criticisms of various writers, and especially because it contains an extensive bibliography which lists all literature by and about Hesse up to 1957. References in German might prove difficult.

Rose, Ernst. *Faith from the Abyss: Hermann Hesse's Way from Romanticism to Modernity.* New York: New York University Press, 1965. One of the most readable works on Hesse, this volume, now in paperback, is excellent in its correlation between biographical incidents and their resultant influence on Hesse's literary production.

Serrano, Miguel. *C. G. Jung and Hermann Hesse: A Record of Two Friendships.* New York: Schoken Books, 1968. This paperback is interesting in its Latin insight into both men by the author, a Chilean diplomat, who was a friend to both. There is, however, little discussion of the relationship between Hesse and Jung.

Wilson, Colin. *The Outsider.* New York: Dell Publishing Co. Inc., 1956. One chapter in this important book, now in paperback, concerns itself with Hesse's protagonists as fringe characters alienated from the mainstream of society.

Zeller, Bernhard. *Portrait of Hesse.* New York: Herder and Herder, 1971. This translation from the German biography is easy to read and provides great insight into its subject. It is also profusely illustrated with interesting photographs.

Ziolkowski, Theodore. *Hermann Hesse.* New York: Columbia University Press, 1966. This pamphlet by the leading Hesse authority provides the best brief overview of Hesse and his works. It places Hesse in perspective as an extremely important writer of the twentieth century.

Ziolkowski, Theodore. *The Novels of Hermann Hesse: A Study in Theme and Structure.* Princeton: Princeton University Press, 1965. This critical masterpiece by Ziolkowski combines thoroughness with easy reading and is extremely interesting. Unfortunately, it deals only with the works from *Demian* to *The Glass Bead Game* (Magister Ludi).

A Hermann Hesse Bibliography for the English-Speaking Student

Writings by Hermann Hesse in English Translation

Peter Camenzind	Farrar, Straus and Giroux Noonday Press
Beneath the Wheel	Farrar, Straus and Giroux Noonday Press Bantam Books
Gertrude	Farrar, Straus and Giroux Noonday Press Bantam Books
Rosshalde	Farrar, Straus and Giroux Noonday Press Bantam Books
Knulp	Farrar, Straus and Giroux Noonday Press
Demian	Harper & Row Bantam Books
Strange News from Another Star	Farrar, Straus and Giroux Noonday Press
Klingsor's Last Summer	Farrar, Straus and Giroux Noonday Press Bantam Books
Wandering	Farrar, Straus and Giroux Noonday Press

Siddhartha	New Directions Bantam Books
Steppenwolf	Holt, Rinehart and Winston Modern Library Bantam Books
Narcissus and Goldmund	Farrar, Straus and Giroux Noonday Press Bantam Books
The Journey to the East	Farrar, Straus and Giroux Noonday Press Bantam Books
The Glass Bead Game (Also published as *Magister Ludi)*	Holt, Rinehart and Winston Bantam Books
If the War Goes On...	Farrar, Straus and Giroux Noonday Press
Poems	Farrar, Straus and Giroux Noonday Press
Autobiographical Writings	Farrar, Straus and Giroux Noonday Press
Stories of Five Decades	Farrar, Straus and Giroux Noonday Press
My Belief	Farrar, Straus and Giroux
Reflections (to be published June 1974)	Farrar, Straus and Giroux
Gerbersau (publication set for late 1974 or 1975)	Farrar, Straus and Giroux
Hesse's Letters (publication set for 1976)	Farrar, Straus and Giroux

I. Books, Pamphlets, and Articles in Books about Hermann Hesse

Andrews, Wayne. "The Achievement of Hermann Hesse," *Siegfried's Curse: The German Journey from Nietzsche to Hesse.* New York: Atheneum, 1972. 274-329.

Barrett, William. "Journey to the East," *In Time of Need: Forms of Imagination in the Twentieth Century.* New York: Harper and Row, 1972. 187-213.

Baumer, Franz. *Hermann Hesse.* New York: Ungar Publishers, 1969.

Boulby, Mark. *Hermann Hesse: His Mind and Art.* Ithaca: Cornell University Press, 1967.

Casebeer, Edwin F. *Hermann Hesse.* New York: Warner Paperback Library, 1972.

Devert, Krystyna. "Hermann Hesse: Apostle of the Apolitical Revolution," *Literature in Revolution.* Edited by George Abbot White and Charles Newman. New York: Holt, Rinehart and Winston, 1972. 302-17.

Engel, Eva J. "Hermann Hesse," *German Men of Letters.* Edited by Alex Natan. London: Oswald Wolff, 1963. Vol. II, 249-74.

Farquharson, Robert H. *An Outline of the Works of Hermann Hesse.* Toronto: Forum House, 1973.

Field, George W. *Hermann Hesse.* New York: Twayne Publishers, 1970.

Fleissner, Else M. *Hermann Hesse: Modern German Poet and Writer.* Charlotteville, New York: Sam-Har Press, 1972.

Freedman, Ralph. *The Lyrical Novel: Studies in Hermann Hesse, Andre Gide and Virginia Woolf.* Princeton: Princeton University Press, 1963.

Friedrichsmeyer, E. S. *Hermann Hesse's "Narcissus and Goldmund": A Critical Commentary.* New York: Monarch Press, 1972.

Glenn, Jerry. *Hermann Hesse's "Siddhartha": A Critical Commentary.* New York: Monarch Press, 1973.

Glenn, Jerry. *The Major Works of Hermann Hesse: A Critical Commentary.* New York: Monarch Press, 1973.

Hanlon, James. "Siddhartha," *Creative Approaches to Reading Literature.* No. 7. Edited by Robert Burns. Middletown, Conn.: Xerox Education Publications, 1974. 97-102.

Hatfield, Henry. "Accepting the Universe: Hermann Hesse's *Steppenwolf,*" *Crisis and Continuity in Modern German Fiction.* Ithaca: Cornell University Press, 1969. 63-77.

Mayer, Hans. "Hermann Hesse's *Steppenwolf,*" *Steppenwolf and Everyman.* Translated by Jack D. Zipes. New York: Thomas Y. Crowell, 1971. 1-13.

Mileck, Joseph. *Hermann Hesse and His Critics.* Chapel Hill: University of North Carolina Press, 1958.

Reichert, Herbert W. *The Impact of Nietzsche on Hermann Hesse.* Mt. Pleasant, Michigan: The Enigma Press, 1972.

Rose, Ernst. *Faith from the Abyss: Hermann Hesse's Way from Romanticism to Modernity.* New York: New York University Press, 1965.

Secundy, Claudia. *Teacher's Guide to Hermann Hesse.* New York: Bantam Books, 1973.

Serrano, Miguel. *C. G. Jung and Hermann Hesse: A Record of Two Friendships.* New York: Schocken Books, 1966.

Simonns, John D. *Hermann Hesse's "Steppenwolf": A Critical Commentary.* New York: Monarch Press, 1972.

Welch, Carolyn R. *"Steppenwolf" and "Siddhartha" Notes.* Lincoln, Nebraska: Cliff's Notes Inc., 1973.

Whiton, John. *Hermann Hesse's "Demian": A Critical Commentary.* New York: Monarch Press, 1973.

Wilson, Colin. *The Outsider.* New York: Dell Publishing Co., 1956. 46-68.

Zeller, Bernhard. *A Portrait of Hesse: An Illustrated Biography.* New York: Herder and Herder, 1971.

Ziolkowski, Theodore. (Ed.) *Hesse: A Collection of Critical Essays.* Englewood Cliffs, New Jersey: Prentice-Hall, Inc., 1973.

_____. *Hermann Hesse.* New York: Columbia University Press, 1965.

_____. "Hesse, Myth, and Reason: Methodological Prolegomena," *Myth and Reason: A Symposium.* Edited by Walter D. Wetzels, Austin: University of Texas Press, 1973. 127-55.

_____. *The Novels of Hermann Hesse: A Study in Theme and Structure.* Princeton: Princeton University Press, 1966.

II. Articles in Periodical Literature about Hermann Hesse

Abood, Edward. "Jung's Concept of Individuation in Hesse's *Steppenwolf." Southern Humanities Review,* 3(1968), 1-13.

Andrews, R. C. "The Poetry of Hermann Hesse," *German Life and Letters* 6 (1952-53), 117-27.

Anolt, V. "Hesse: An Existential Thinker," *Contemporary Education*, 44 (Feb., 1973), 212-14.

Bandy, Stephen C. "Hermann Hesse's *Glasperlenspiel:* In Search of Joseph Knecht," *Modern Language Quarterly*, 33(Sept. 1972), 299-331.

Bauke, Joseph P. "Narcissus and Goldmund," *Saturday Review of Literature*, 51(May 4, 1968) 32-33.

Beerman, Hans. "Hermann Hesse and the Bhagavad-Gita," *Midwest Quarterly*, I(1959), 27-40.

Benn, Maurice. "An Interpretation of the Work of Hermann Hesse," *German Life and Letters*, 3(1949-50), 202-11.

Boulby, Mark. "Der Vierte Lebenslauf as a Key to *Das Glasperlenspiel*," *Modern Language Review*, 61(1966), 635-46.

Bretensky, Dennis. "*Siddhartha:* A Casebook on Teaching Methods," *English Journal*, 62(March, 1973), 379-82.

Bronson, John. "Death and the Lover," *Bookman*, 76(June, 1933), 91-92.

Butler, Colin. "Hermann Hesse's *Siddhartha:* Some Critical Objections," *Monatshefte*, 63(1971), 117-24.

_____. "Literary Malpractice in Some Works of Hermann Hesse," *University of Toronto Quarterly*, 40(1971), 168-82.

Cohn, Dorrit. "Narration of Consciousness in *Der Steppenwolf*," *Germanic Review*, 44(March, 1969), 121-31.

Cohn, Hilde. "The Symbolic End of Hermann Hesse's *Glasperlenspiel*," *Modern Language Quarterly*, 11(1950), 347-57.

Colby, Thomas. "The Impenitent Prodigal: Hermann Hesse's Hero," *German Quarterly*, 40(1967), 14-23.

Crenshaw, Karen O. and Lawson, Richard H. "Technique and Function of Time in Hesse's *Morgenlandfahrt:* A Culmination," *Mosaic* (Spring-Summer, 1972), 53-59.

Engel, Monroe. "Magister Ludi," *Nation*, 169(Dec. 24, 1949), 626-27.

Enright, D. J. "Hesse vs. Hesse," *New York Review of Books*, (Sept. 12, 1968), 10.

Farquharson, Robert H. "The Identity and Significance of Leo in Hesse's *Morgenlandfahrt*," *Monatshefte*, 55(1963), 122-28.

Farrelly, John. "Demian," *New Republic*, 118(Feb. 23, 1948), 24.

Fickert, Kurt J. "The Development of the Outsider Concept in Hesse's Novels," *Monatshefte*, 52(1960), 171-78.

Field, G. W. "Hermann Hesse: A Neglected Nobel Prize Novelist," *Queen's Quarterly*, 65(1958), 514-20.

_____. "Hermann Hesse as Critic of English and American Literature," *Monatshefte*, 53(1961), 147-58.

_____. "Music and Morality in Thomas Mann and Hermann Hesse," *University of Toronto Quarterly*, 24(1955), 175-90.

_____. "On the Genesis of Hesse's *Glasperlenspiel*," *German Quarterly*, 41(1968), 673-88.

Flaxman, Seymour H. "*Der Steppenwolf:* Hesse's Portrait of the Intellectual," *Modern Language Quarterly*, 15(1954), 349-58.

Foran, Marion. "Hermann Hesse," *Queen's Quarterly*, 55(May 9, 1948), 180-89.

Ford, Richard J. "Hermann Hesse: Prophet of the Pot Generation," *Catholic World*, 212(Oct. 1970), 15-19.

Freemantle, Anne. "Good and Evil: *Demian*," *New York Herald
Tribune Weekly Book Review*, (Feb. 29, 1948), 27.

Freedman, Ralph. "Hermann Hesse," *Contemporary Literature*,
10(Summer, 1969), 421-26.

_____. "Romantic Imagination: Hermann Hesse as a Modern
Novelist," *Publication of the Modern Language Association*,
73(June, 1958), 275-84.

Goldgar, Harry. "Hesse's *Glasperlenspiel* and the Game of Go,"
German Life and Letters, 20(1966), 132-37.

Goldman, Albert. *"The Glass Bead Game:* Fanned by Youth,"
Vogue, 155(Jan. 1, 1970), 82.

Gowan, B. "Demian," *Monatshefte*, 20(1928), 225-28.

Gropper, Esther C. "Literature for the Restive: Hermann Hesse's
Books," *English Journal*, 59(Dec., 1970), 1226-28.

_____. "The Disenchanted Turn to Hesse," *English Journal*,
61(Oct. 1972), 979-84.

Gross, Harvey. "Hermann Hesse," *Western Review*, 17(1953),
132-40.

Hallamore, Joyce. "Paul Klee, H. H. and *Die Morgenlandfahrt*,"
Seminar, 1(1965), 17-24.

Halpert, Inge. "The Alt Musikmeister and Goethe," *Monatshefte*,
52(1960), 159-64.

_____. "Vita Activa and Vita Contemplativa," *Monatshefte*,
53(1961), 159-66.

Halsband, R. "Siddhartha," *Saturday Review of Literature*,
(Dec. 22, 1951), 38.

Hanlon, James. "Siddhartha," *Senior Paperbacks*, (April, 1973), 3-4.

Heller, Peter. "The Creative Unconscious and the Spirit: A Study of Polarities in Hesse's Image of the Writer," *Modern Language Forum*, 38(1953), 28-40.

_____. "The Masochistic Rebel in Recent German Literature," *Journal of Aesthetics and Art Criticism*, 2(1953), 205-6.

_____. "The Writer in Conflict With His Age: A Study in the Ideology of Hermann Hesse," *Monatshefte*, 46(1954), 137-47.

Hill, Claude. "Hermann Hesse and Germany," *German Quarterly*, 21(1948), 9-15.

_____. "Herr Hesse and the Modern Neurosis: *Steppenwolf*," *New York Times Book Review*, (March 16, 1947), 5.

_____. "The Journey to the East," *Saturday Review of Literature*, (June, 1957), 12.

Hirsch, T. E. "Demian," *Library Journal*, 72(1947), 1685.

Hughes, Kenneth. "Hesse's Use of Gilgamesh Motifs in the Humanization of Siddhartha and Harry Haller," *Seminar*, 5(1969), 129-40.

Irvine, L. "Steppenwolf," *Athenaeum*, (May 11, 1929), 208.

Jaeger, Hans. "Heidegger's Existential Philosophy and Modern German Literature," *Publication of the Modern Language Association*, 67(1952), 655.

Jehle, Mimi. "The 'Garden' in the Works of Hermann Hesse," *German Quarterly*, 24(1951), 42-50.

Johnson, Sidney H. "The Autobiographies in Hermann Hesse's *Glasperlenspiel*," *German Quarterly*, 29(1956), 160-71.

Koch, Stephen. "Prophet of Youth," *New Republic*, 159(July 13, 1968), 23-26.

Koester, Rudolf. "Hermann Hesse: Portrayal of Age in Hesse's Narrative Prose," *Germanic Review*, 61(March, 1966), 111-19.

_____. "Hesse's Music Master: In Search of a Prototype," *Forum for Modern Language Studies*, 3(1967), 135-41.

_____. "Self-Realization: Reflections on Youth," *Monatshefte*, 57(1965), 181-86.

Kronenberger, Louis. "Death and the Lover," *New York Herald Tribune Books*, (Dec. 11, 1932), 18.

Lazare, Christopher. "A Measure of Wisdom: *Siddhartha*," *New York Times Book Review*, (Dec. 2, 1951), 52.

Lesser, J. "Hermann Hesse: Nobel Prize Winner," *The Contemporary Review*, 171(1947), 31-34.

MacDonald, Dwight. "Books," *New Yorker*, (Jan. 23, 1954), 98.

Malthaner, J. "A Visit with Hermann Hesse," *Books Abroad*, 21(1947), 146-52.

_____. "Herman Hesse: *Siddhartha*," *German Quarterly*, 25(1952), 103-9.

Maurer, Warren R. "Jean Paul and Hermann Hesse: Katzenbergen and Kurgast," *Seminar*, 4(1968), 113-28.

Middleton, Drew. "A Literary Letter from Germany," *New York Times Book Review*, (July 31, 1949), 2.

Middleton, J. C. "An Enigma Transfigured in Hermann Hesse's *Glasperlenspiel*," *German Life and Letters*, 10(1956-57), 298-302.

_____. "Hermann Hesse's *Morgenlandfahrt*," *Germanic Review*, 32(1957), 299-310.

Mihailovich, Vasa D. "Hermann Hesse as a Critic of Russian Literature," *Arcadia*, 2(1967), 91-102.

Mileck, Joseph. "A Visit with Hermann Hesse and a Journey from Montagnola to Calw," *Modern Language Forum*, 41(1956), 3-8.

_____. *"Das Glasperlenspiel:* Genesis, Manuscripts, and History of Publication," *German Quarterly*, 43(1970), 55-83.

_____. "Hesse Bibliography," *Monatshefte*, 49(1957), 201-5.

_____. "Hesse Collections in Europe," *Monatshefte*, 47(1955), 290-94.

_____. "Hermann Hesse and Romain Rolland: Briefe," *Modern Language Notes*, 70(1955), 627.

_____. "Hermann Hesse's *Glasperlenspiel*," *University of California Publications in Modern Philology*, 36(1952), 243-70.

_____. "Names and the Creative Process," *Monatshefte*, 53(1961), 167-80.

_____. "The Poetry of Hermann Hesse," *Monatshefte,* 66(1954), 192-98.

_____. "The Prose of Hermann Hesse: Life, Substance, and Form," *German Quarterly*, 27(1954), 163-74.

Misra, Bhábagrahi. "An Analysis of the Indic Tradition in Hermann Hesse's *Siddhartha*," *Indian Literature*, 11(1968), 111-23.

Morris, A. S. "The Will to Perish: Demian," *New York Times Book Review*, (Feb. 1, 1948), 6.

Mueller, Gustav. "A Hermann Hesse Reminiscence," *Books Abroad*, 21(1947), 287.

_____. "Hermann Hesse," *Books Abroad*, 21(1947), 146-52.

Naumann, Walter. "The Individual and Society in the Works of Hermann Hesse," *Monatshefte*, 41(1949), 33-42.

Negus, Kenneth. "On the Death of Joseph Knecht in Hermann Hesse's *Glasperlenspiel*," *Monatshefte*, 53(1961), 181-89.

Norton, Roger C. "Hermann Hesse's Criticism of Technology," *Germanic Review*, 43(1968), 267-73.

_____. "Variant Endings of Hesse's *Glasperlenspiel*," *Monatshefte*, 60(1968), 141-46.

Park, C. W. "Notes on Hermann Hesse's Verse," *Poetry*, 70(1947), 206-8.

Pasinetti, P. H. "Novels from Three Languages," *Sewanee Review*, 56(1948), 171-4.

Paslick, Robert H. "Dialectic and Non-Attachment: The Structure of Hermann Hesse's *Siddhartha*," *Symposium*, (Spring, 1973), 67-75.

Pawel, Ernst. "Stories of Five Decades," *New York Times Book Review*, (Feb. 11, 1973), 7.

Peppard, Murray. "Hermann Hesse's Ladder of Learning," *Kentucky Foreign Language Quarterly*, 3(1956), 13-20.

Peters, Eric. "Hermann Hesse: The Psychological Implications of His Writings," *German Life and Letters*, 1(1948), 209-14.

Pick, Robert. "Cryptic Game of Beads," *Saturday Review of Literature*, (Oct. 15, 1949), 15-16.

_____. "Demian," *Saturday Review of Literature,* (Jan. 24, 1948), 18.

_____. "Nobel Prize Winner Hesse," *Saturday Review of Literature,* (Dec. 7, 1946), 38-40.

Plant, Richard. "Magister Ludi," *New York Times Book Review,* (Oct. 30, 1944), 52.

Porterfield, A. W. "Mozart Still Lives: *Steppenwolf,*" *New York Herald Tribune Books,* (Sept. 8, 1929), 4.

Resnik, Henry S. "How Hermann Hesse Speaks to the College Generation," *Saturday Review,* 52(Oct. 18, 1969), 35-37.

Sammons, Jeffrey. "Notes on the Germanization of American Youth," *The Yale Review,* (Spring, 1970), 342-56.

Schludermann, Brigette. "Mythical Reflections of the East in Hermann Hesse," *Mosaic,* 2(1968/69), 97-111.

Schneider, Christian I. "Loss of Soul Without Nature," *National Parks and Conservation Magazine,* 44(August, 1970), 20.

Schwarz, Egon. "Hermann Hesse: The American Youth Movement, and Problems of Literary Evaluation," *Publication of the Modern Language Association,* 85(October, 1970), 977-87.

Seidlin, Oscar. "Hermann Hesse: Exorcism of the Demon," *Symposium,* (Nov. 1950), 325-48.

_____. "Hermann Hesse's *Glasperlenspiel,*" *Germanic Review,* 23(1948), 263-73.

Shaw, Leroy. "Time and the Structure of Hermann Hesse's *Siddhartha,*" *Symposium,* 11(1957), 204-24.

Shuster, G. W. "A Comment on the Soul of an Artist," *New York Herald Tribune Book Review,* (March 16, 1947), 1.

Sklar, Robert. "Tolkien and Hesse: Top of the Pops," *Nation*, 204(May 8, 1967), 598-601.

Smith, B. "Steppenwolf," *New York World*, (Oct. 27, 1929), 11.

Stanck, Lou Willett. "Hesse and Moffett Team-Teach the Theory of Discourse," *English Journal*, 61(Oct. 1972), 985-93.

Steiner, G. "Eastward Ho!" *New Yorker*, 44(Jan. 18, 1969), 87-90.

Taylor, R. "Steppenwolf," *Spectator*, (May 18, 1929), 290-93.

Timpe, Eugene F. "Hermann Hesse in the United States," *Symposium*, 23(Spring, 1969), 73-79.

———. "Hesse's Siddhartha and the Bhagavad-Gita," *Comparative Literature*, 22(Fall, 1970), 346-57.

Townsend, S. "The German Humanist Hermann Hesse," *Modern Language Forum*, 32(1947), 1-12.

Vonnegut, Kurt Jr. "Why They Read Hesse," *Horizon*, 12(Spring, 1970), 28-31.

Werner, Alfred. "Nobel Prize Winner," *New York Times Book Review*, (Dec. 8, 1946), 56-57.

———. "Hermann Hesse," *South Atlantic Quarterly*, 52(July, 1958), 384-90.

Weyr, Thomas. "Hermann Hesse and the American German Review," *American German Review*, 35:2(1969), 1.

Wilson, A. L. "Hesse's Veil of Isis," *Monatshefte*, 55(1963), 313-21.

Wood, Ralph Charles. "Hermann Hesse," *American German Review*, 43(1956), 3-6.

Ziolkowski, Theodore. "Hesse's Sudden Popularity with To-day's Students," *University: Princeton Quarterly*, (Summer, 1970), 19-25.

_____. "Hermann Hesse's Chiliastic Vision," *Monatshefte*, 53(1961), 199-210.

_____. "Saint Hesse Among the Hippies," *American Germanic Review*, 35:2(1969), 19-23.

Miscellaneous Articles about Hermann Hesse

"A God Within," *Time*, 86(July 30, 1965), 68-69.

"Hermann Hesse's *Briefe*," *The Times Literary Supplement*, (Dec. 28, 1951), 838.

"The Novels of Hermann Hesse," *The Times Literary Supplement*, (Dec. 19, 1952), 835.

"Outsider," *Time*, 92(Oct. 18, 1968), 111-12.

"Siddhartha," *Nation*, (Nov. 17, 1951), 430.

"Steppenwolf," *Bookman*, (Oct. 1924), xxii.

"Teaching Guide for *Siddhartha*," *Campus Book Club Publication*, (Jan. 1974), 2-3.

"The Wolf Man," *New York Times Book Review*, (Sept. 29, 1929), 7.

NOTES

NOTES